Cryptocurrency Trading For Beginners

6-Steps Action Plan To Your First Investment

Kate C.

Introduction

What if someone ask you if it's too late to invest in Apple or Google?

If you had invested $1000 in Apple Inc. stock in 2002, you would have gained 50 times your investment at $50000+. At this point of writing Apple Inc is at $179 and has already touched $9 billion market cap.

Most of us don't have the time, money or luxury to invest like Warren Buffet or George Soros let alone wait sixteen years for another opportunity like Apple or Google to appear. To make matters worse, our modern life is often characterized by busy work life demands leaving us little or no time to do the most important thing which is to invest for our retirement.

But the rise of cryptocurrency has shown us there is a new way! It is now your time to seize this opportunity while many have stayed on the sidelines because they are too lazy or fear the unknown and did not take the time to understand the depth of cryptocurrency beyond just being a digital cash system.

In this book, you will be shown a simple action plan to start your first cryptocurrency trading journey with as little as $50-100.

Whether you're a beginner or experienced trader, you'll benefit from the easy to follow steps which have allowed many to consistently generate positive revenue without spending too much time and effort navigating in the confusing world of cryptocurrency.

If you follow the steps in this book, you'll invest smart and not follow others blindly or be shaken by bad news. Others will be wondering how it's possible you got so much done in so little time while still holding a day job. As a bonus you'll end up having more money, time and energy to focus on what is truly important to you while building your retirement nest.

Don't live your life sitting on the fence when for just the price of a cup of coffee you can start taking action now and transform yourself into a savvy cryptocurrency trader before the rest of the world catches up onto this golden opportunity.

Scroll up to the top and Click Buy Now.

Table of Contents

Introduction   **3**

Chapter 1: Is It Too Late To Invest In Cryptocurrency or Bitcoin?   **9**

    Are Cryptocurrencies In A Bubble?   9

    Why It Is Not Too Late To Invest In Cryptocurrencies and Bitcoin   10

Chapter 2: Cryptocurrency Basics   **13**

    What Is Cryptocurrency?   13

    What Is Bitcoin?   17

    What Is Ethereum?   19

    Main Difference Between Bitcoin And Ethereum   21

    Coins, Tokens And Altcoins - What's The Difference?   21

Chapter 3: Initial Coin Offerings (ICOs) Basics   **23**

    What Is Initial Coin Offerings (ICOs)?   23

    How Do ICOs Work?   23

    Difference Between ICOs and IPOs   24

    Why Invest In ICOs?   25

Chapter 4: 6-Steps Action Plan To Your First Investment   **27**

    Step 1: Source For Potential ICOs   27

    Step 2: Research Of ICOs   28

    Step 3: ICOs Analysis Checklist   30

    Step 4: Opening Of Cryptocurrency Exchange Account   35

    Step 5: How To Send Your BTC or ETH To ICOs   45

    Step 6: Post ICOs   51

Chapter 5: Case Studies - The Good, The Bad And The Ugly   **55**

Case Study 1 - The "Good"	55
Case Study 2 - The "Bad"	57
Case Study 3 - The "Ugly"	59

Chapter 6: Risk Management & Trading Psychology 63

Risk Management	63
Trading Psychology	67

Chapter 7: Bonus 71

Types Of Crypto Wallets	71
How To Transfer Coins	73

Conclusion 77

Useful Resources 79

Text Copyright © 2018 Kate C.

All rights reserved. No part of this guide may be reproduced in any form without permission in writing from the publisher except in the case of brief quotations embodied in critical articles or reviews.

Legal & Disclaimer

The information contained or provided in this book is not intended to be and does not constitute financial advice, investment advice, trading advice or any other advice. It is not meant to replace the need for independent financial, legal or other professional advice or services, as may be required. The content and information in this book has been provided for educational and entertainment purposes only.

The content and information contained in this book has been compiled from sources deemed reliable, and it is accurate to the best of the Author's knowledge, information and belief. However, the Author cannot guarantee its accuracy and validity and cannot be held liable for any errors and/or omissions. Further, changes are periodically made to this book as and when needed.

Upon using the contents and information contained in this book, you agree to hold harmless the Author from and against any damages, costs, and expenses, including any legal fees potentially resulting from the application of any of the information provided by this book. This disclaimer applies to any loss, damages or injury caused by the use and application, whether directly or indirectly, of any advice or information presented, whether for breach of contract, tort, negligence, personal injury, criminal intent, or under any other cause of action.

You agree to accept all risks of using the information presented inside this book.

You agree that by continuing to read this book, where appropriate and/or necessary, you shall consult a professional (including but not limited to your attorney, or financial advisor or such other advisor as needed) before using any of the suggested techniques, or information in this book.

Chapter 1:
Is It Too Late To Invest In Cryptocurrency or Bitcoin?

The reason people ask if it is too late to invest in cryptocurrency and Bitcoin is because they are not sure if it is here to stay. Most people only heard of Bitcoin recently because of its high prices ($14121 at this point of writing). Bitcoin actually started in 2009 and virtual currencies have been around much longer.

Similar to how:

-Airbnb is disrupting the hospitality market,

-Uber and Lyft disrupting the taxi market,

-Facebook disrupting the content market,

-Alibaba and Amazon disrupting the retail market

Cryptocurrencies and Bitcoin are now disrupting the financial markets and are here to stay.

Are Cryptocurrencies In A Bubble?

This is the second most popular and burning question relating to investing in cryptocurrencies as some people think cryptocurrencies' quick rise over the past year means that they are overvalued.

If you look in perspective to the US stock market at $25 Trillion, the entire size of the cryptocurrency market cap at $524B is merely a fraction of it. Apple Inc. alone has already passed $900B and Alphabet Inc aka Google at $771B. Both companies alone are bigger than the entire cryptocurrency market cap.

The fact that the entire cryptocurrency market cap is not even larger than some top Fortune 500 companies means there is still room to scale.

Why It Is Not Too Late To Invest In Cryptocurrencies and Bitcoin

Now let's take a look at the historical data of Bitcoin and see what you have missed out.

For example 1 Bitcoin in Nov 2017 was $8,244.69

If you bought 1 Bitcoin (BTC):

-3 months earlier: 1 BTC @ $4,066.60 = 103% return

-6 months earlier: 1 BTC @ $2,040.18 = 304% return

-12 months earlier: 1 BTC $728.51 = 1032% return

Let's look at the No. 2 coin Ethereum.

For example 1 Ethereum in Nov 2017 was $367.71

If you bought 1 Ethereum (ETH):

-3 months earlier: 1 ETH @ $298.20 = 23% return

-6 months earlier: 1 ETH @ $123.06 = 199% return

-12 months earlier: 1 ETH @ $9.57 = 3742% return

Nobody can predict if these upward trends will continue. But the point is the longer you sit on the fence, the more you are going to wish you got in earlier. Even if you started three months ago, you would still be making great returns.

By the way if you are still asking "Is it too late to get into cryptocurrency?" The answer is "No, it is not too late to get into cryptocurrency today".

Note: All prices in this book are in USD.

Chapter 2: Cryptocurrency Basics

What Is Cryptocurrency?

Cryptocurrencies are a digital form of currency known as virtual currencies, digital cash or tokens but not like your regular USD or British pounds as they are not backed by any government. Cryptocurrencies are more like the digital equivalent of gold because like gold they are in limited amounts held in a decentralized system which means no one can "print" more of it or "take it down". Do you know there will only be 21 million Bitcoins to be released? It is estimated only 4.3 million Bitcoins are left.

Each cryptocurrency such as Bitcoin is an encrypted decentralized virtual currency transferred between peers, whereby all transactions are confirmed through a mining process and recorded in a public ledger.

1. You send 1 BTC to Sam's e-wallet address.

3. Sam receive 1 BTC on his e-wallet.

2. Network of peers / miners confirms the transaction and are rewarded new coins.

For example, when you send Bitcoin to your friend Sam, you are creating a transaction into a special type of database that is shared via a peer-to-peer network (think BitTorrent). This network does not rely on a central server or authority but it ensures you can't send the same Bitcoin twice to Sam and Kelly, because every peer has a complete record of the history of all entries made within the network thus preventing "double-spending". This entire history known as public ledger includes the balance of all accounts including yours. The innovation of cryptocurrency is its ability to achieve all these without a central server or authority like banks or institutions.

Cryptocurrencies are generated by the network to incentivize the peers often known as miners or nodes who work to secure network and confirm transactions by solving complex mathematical puzzles. For example, Bitcoin rewards the miners with a small transaction fee along with newly created coins for "solving the next block" whereby the term "blockchain" came from.

Mining Hardware

Note: Mining is open source, so anyone can be a miner with the right software, specialized hardware (ATI graphics processing unit - GPU ranging from $90-$3000), online mining pool membership and reliable internet connection.

Bitcoin, Ethereum, Litecoin, Ripple are currently among the top cryptocurrencies. At this point of writing there are 1384 coins and still growing. Every cryptocurrency is a little different but most share these basic characteristics:

- One-way and irreversible with no chargeback. You can't retrieve it once the network confirmed your cryptocurrency was sent.

- Anonymous as anyone can open an online wallet without any ID.

- Fast and globally accessible as entries are broadcast across the network immediately and confirmed within a few minutes.

- Controlled limited supply by the network. E.g. there is only 21 million Bitcoins created.

What Is Bitcoin?

Bitcoin (BTC) is a cryptocurrency and the first decentralized digital currency that works without a central bank or single administrator. It is also a payment network that facilitates the movement of value represented as Bitcoin worldwide. Transactions are made without middle men. Instead it uses a peer-to-peer network to verify transactions through miners who are rewarded with small transaction fees along with newly created Bitcoins.

Bitcoin was invented and released as an open-source software in 2009 by a person or group with the pseudonym Satoshi Nakamoto. It was conceived at the wake of the Great Recession of 2007-2008 (triggered by the collapse of the housing bubble in the U.S. which led to the collapse of Lehman Brothers). The ideology behind Bitcoin is to shift the power away from the government and big banks to the masses in the form of decentralized empowerment to prevent their control which had resulted in adverse consequences to the economy and society. To know more you can read the original Bitcoin White Paper here: https://bitcoin.org/bitcoin.pdf

Note: If you had bought $1000 worth of Bitcoin in 2010, you will be worth $35 million today!

What Is Ethereum?

Ethereum (ETH) is the second biggest coin after Bitcoin. In the beginning of 2017 the price of Ethereum grew from $7 to $1252 in Jan 2018.

Ethereum is not just a digital currency but also a decentralized software platform and programming language. It is renowned for its Smart Contracts and Distributed Applications (DApps). Developers can build and deploy a wide range of decentralized applications powered by its Smart Contracts (which are self-executing programmable codes). Smart contracts can be used to exchange funds, shares, property, insurance, business contracts, crowdfunding agreements or anything of value in a transparent conflict-free way without a middleman.

For example you can rent a house from anyone in the world using a virtual contract of which it will only release the funds if the contract is fulfilled at the set time, otherwise it will automatically be canceled. This safeguards both parties until the deal is realized and also saves the usual 6-12% fees paid to a middleman like Airbnb.

Note: Ethereum Classic (ETC) is different from Ethereum (ETH). ETC was the original chain which had remained as Ethereum Classic due to ideological disagreement with the new chain (ETH). From a user's perspective it is vital to use the new ETH platform as it has an active development team for the latest updates, supervision and enhancement.

Main Difference Between Bitcoin And Ethereum

Bitcoin is purely a digital currency while Ethereum aims to expand the use of blockchain technology by including other applications besides transferring of value. Imagine Bitcoin as a smartphone app that does only one function while Ethereum works like an app store whereby other developers can create new applications using their platform.

Coins, Tokens And Altcoins - What's The Difference?

All coins and tokens are regarded as cryptocurrencies. The two common categorizations are:

1. **Alternative Cryptocurrency Coins (Altcoins)** are any alternative cryptocurrency coins besides Bitcoin. Majority of altcoins are a variant of Bitcoin and built using Bitcoin's open sourced original protocol. Examples of Bitcoins variants are Litecoin, Namecoin, Peercoin, Dogecoin and Auroracoin. Namecoin was the first Altcoin created in 2011.

Ethereum, Waves, Omni, Nxt and Ripple are some of the other Altcoins that use their own blockchain and protocol instead of Bitcoin's.

2. **Tokens** usually reside on top of another blockchain as a representative of a particular asset or utility. Tokens can represent any assets that are fungible and tradeable from loyalty points to commodities. Tokens can be created using a standard template on Ethereum or Waves platform and made functional through the use of smart contracts.

For example at a theme park, you gave your money (Ether) and they gave you a band (Token) around your wrist to gain access to all the rides. Or when you pay money (Ether) for your movie, you receive a ticket (Token) to get into the cinema theater.

The main difference between altcoins and tokens: altcoins are separate currencies with their own blockchain while tokens operate on top of a blockchain that facilitates the creation of decentralized applications.

Chapter 3: Initial Coin Offerings (ICOs) Basics

What Is Initial Coin Offerings (ICOs)?

Initial Coin Offerings (ICOs) are basically crowd sales and the cryptocurrency version of crowdfunding via the creation and sale of digital coins or tokens to fund project development.

One of the things that makes Ethereum special and fuels its growth from $7 to $1252 in one year is the rise of Initial Coin Offerings (ICOs). Most crypto backed startups raise millions in a matter of days through ICOs. Almost all of these projects leverage on Ethereum to build their applications and issue their native currency. As such you will usually need Ethereum tokens (ETH) to invest in ICOs in exchange for their native tokens.

How Do ICOs Work?

A developer will issue a limited amount of tokens as this will ensure the tokens themselves have a value and the ICO has a target to aim for example $10 million. The tokens can have a pre-determined price, example 1 ETH = 7000 tokens or increase / decrease depending on the crowd sale response.

If you want to buy tokens and take part, you just have to send a particular amount of ether (ETH) to the crowd sale address. Once the transaction is done, you will receive your corresponding amount of tokens, for example your investment of 1 ETH will give you 7000 tokens for that particular ICO.

An ICO is considered successful if it is properly well-distributed and a majority of it not owned by one entity e.g. "whales" who can control the market with their large coin holdings.

Difference Between ICOs and IPOs

IPOs (Initial Public Offerings) refers to the public sale of shares of a company for the first time with the goal to raise funds for its business development and expansion. Let's look at the difference:

IPOs:

- Only established companies with a track record can offer IPOs

- Follows strict regulatory environment with multiple applications to relevant authorities such as Securities and Exchange Commission (SEC)

- Promises to share dividends from company profits

- Offering is exclusive, by invite only

ICOs:

- A new startup with no ready product in the market, can use ICO to raise funds

- No existing regulatory requirements and anyone can launch an ICO and invite the public to buy using white papers to describe and propose their product or business ideas

- Tokens don't offer dividends, only a promise its price will grow and the investor can sell to profit

- Offering is open to all

Why Invest In ICOs?

From Jan to July 2017 a staggering US$1,252,676,352 was raised in ICOs. One such ICO - Basic attention Token (BAT) raised $35 million in 35 seconds!

Let's take a look at the actual ROI (Return On Investment) of some ICOs since inception:

Taken on Jan 2018:

- Chainlink: $100 investment will give you $1254 at 12.54%

- BAT: $100 investment will give you $2410 at 24.10%

- Ethereum: $100 investment will give you $390559 at 3905.59%

- NXT: $100 investment will give you $3016805 at 30168.05%!

Note: You can refer to all the ROI since ICO at https://icostats.com/roi-since-ico

As you can see, the returns generated from investing ICOs is huge. However since ICOs are not regulated, there are also many Ponzi-like scams or MLM if you are not careful. In the next chapter we will begin our action plan to investing your first ICO using thorough fundamental analysis and due diligence to sieve out the rogue ones.

Chapter 4: 6-Steps Action Plan To Your First Investment

Step 1: Source For Potential ICOs

Here are the recommended resources to find upcoming ICOs:

- Crush Crypto: https://crushcrypto.com/

- Smith & Crown: https://www.smithandcrown.com/

- ICO Alert: https://www.icoalert.com/

- Reddit Channels: /r/Cryptocurrency and /r/icocrypto

Of the above Crush Crypto is my top choice for sourcing upcoming ICOs. Under their analysis section they provide detailed analysis on selected upcoming ICOs. These analyses include summary, project overview, pros and cons and a short video summary for those who prefer to watch rather than read. The best part is they are often spot-on on promising ICOs. For starters this is a great resource to begin and familiarize yourself with the ins and outs of ICOs analysis as well as how to spot a good or bad ICO.

Step 2: Research Of ICOs

Once you have spotted a potential ICO, it is time to practice due diligence with research and fundamental analysis to evaluate its worthiness as a good investment for your money.

Remember ICOs are unlike traditional investments such as stocks; we cannot rely on any numbers, past track record or even a working product to make our investment decision.

Note:

- ICOs are not corporations but representations of value or assets within a network (there's no promise of dividends from profit sharing)

- Almost all ICOs are either in infancy or development stage (there's no track record or past performance to show)

As such our fundamental analysis will focus on assessing the viability and potential of coins which means the potential price will grow so you as the investor can sell to profit.

Understanding The ICO / Coin You Are Investing In

Once you understand the coin's fundamentals, you can form your own opinions about it and be confident of your investment. Here's where and what to look for when assessing ICO / coin:

a) **ICO / Coin's White Paper**

This is a detailed proposal by the development team outlining the purpose and mechanics of the coin. This represents your main source of evaluating the coin's fundamentals. White Paper can range from 1 to 50 pages and can get very technical because of its technological jargon and concepts. However a technical white paper is a good sign compared to a sales or gimmicky white paper (which might be a scam).

Tip: If you find the white paper too technical, you can try looking for the one-page condensed version on the ICO website, Crushcrypto.com or forums.

b) **ICO / Coin's Slack Channel or Blog**

This represents the development team's official channel of communication and news of updates with the public. Join their slack channel or blog to follow the interaction and questions raised to get more insider information on the coin.

c) **Forums**

Reddit, Bitcointalk and Steemit forums are great resources to understand the coins / ICOs better as you will see the public sentiments surrounding the project e.g. Are people excited about the ICO? These forums are also a good resource if you like to learn more or find simpler explanations about cryptocurrency.

Tip: Type "EL15" (Explain it to me like I'm 5 years old) in your search query to find simple definitions for unfamiliar technical jargon.

Note: For convenience you can download Slack, Reddit and Telegram on your smartphone to follow news and updates from the ICOs you are interested in.

Useful Resources:

1) Reddit - https://www.reddit.com

2) Steemit - https://steemit.com

3) BitcoinForum - https://bitcointalk.org

Step 3: ICOs Analysis Checklist

Most of the answers can be found on the ICO website.

Q1. What does the coin / project do?

This is to assess if the coin has a clear objective. Is it the first of its kind? Who is their closest competitor and how far along are they?

Q2. Does it solve a real problem with real customers?

This is to assess if the coin offers a practical solution to real world problems with a well-defined target market. The solution has to be viable in the long term to be profitable.

Q3. Does the coin / token have any utility?

Utility refers to the central function of a service. A coin with a strong utility will incentivize people to hold it as an investment and increase its value e.g. Ethereum platform.

Q4. Is the white paper written like a technical textbook or marketing gimmick?

If it is written like an infomercial or sounds too good to be true, it might be a scam. For white paper you want to see boring technical details as it is supposed to be geeky. There have been cases whereby some even copied other ICO's white paper with minimal changes.

Q5. Who are the team members behind the coin / project?

The success of a project really depends on a solid team. Ideally the founding team should consist of experienced members and engineers with relevant background. It is even better if they are supported by prominent investors or well known credible advisors. E.g. the team shouldn't be made up of 7 marketing staff and their only engineer is a college student working part time.

Q6. How advanced is the project?

Is there any working product to show? E.g. A running software or platform on alpha or beta to prove it works.

Q7. Do they have a clear roadmap or timeline of the project development?

How are the development stages of the project planned out? Is it over a year or two? Are they active in updating the progress of the project on forums or their website? This will give you a good indication of how long the project will take to come to fruition. It also shows the team commitment to see the project through.

Q8. How much money has been raised or spent?

You want to see prudent handling of funds by the development team. The more specific they are the better it is.

Q9. Does it face any possible legal barriers?

Some industries might require strict regulations resulting in delays and additional legal costs.

Q10. How many coins will be issued?

A fixed supply of coins means the value of the coin will likely increase in proportion e.g. there are only 21 million Bitcoins ever. A supply that isn't fixed means it might not sustain a price growth over time.

Q11. Is there a hard cap on the coin / project?

A hard cap meaning maximum amount can be anything from $1 to $25 million. This determines the total initial issuance of coins / tokens to be created. A hard cap will bring more value to investors as compared to no-cap which means supply is not limited.

Q12. How much will the founders get?

The average benchmark is 10-20% for the founding team as you do not want them to manipulate the prices with their share.

Q13. How long is the lock up period?

Lock up period means the founders cannot sell their coins within a timeframe. The longer the better as it means they will be committed to see the project through.

Tip: You can also use the above checklist to help you assess any cryptocurrency coins, tokens and ICOs.

Red Flags: Spotting Scams, MLM, Pyramid And Ponzi Schemes

How To Spot Scams

The easiest way to check for scam warnings relating to the coin / project is to use our good friend Google. Do a quick search on Google e.g. "FuzeX ICO" and scan through the results. If you spot a few sources citing the coin / project as a scam, you might want to stay away.

How To Spot A MLM Or Pyramid Scheme

MLM (Multi Level Marketing) or Pyramid schemes often results in only the top level management being paid handsomely. The nature of cryptocurrency should be backed by blockchain technology not MLM.

How To Spot A Ponzi Scheme

The telltale sign of a Ponzi scheme is offering fixed daily or monthly returns which is not what blockchain technology is about.

Recap:

Make full use of the checklist above and practice due diligence when deciding on which coin / project to invest in. If you do not understand the value of your coin / project and invest on hearsay it is not much difference from gambling. Lastly, if you have the slightest doubt about the coin / project's integrity, it is best to give it a pass as there are plenty of better qualified ICOs for your dollar.

Tip: A good way to start and familiarize yourself with investing in ICOs is via paper trading (virtual trading) till you feel confident with your acumen.

Step 4: Opening Of Cryptocurrency Exchange Account

Cryptocurrency exchanges are websites where you can buy, sell or exchange cryptocurrencies for fiat money (paper money) or crypto coins.

Due to the increasing popularity of cryptocurrency, the opening of an exchange account is taking noticeably longer than usual with some popular exchanges like Bittrex halting new account openings. Therefore do start the process as soon as possible as the verification process can sometimes take a few weeks and you will need time to submit personal information such as your passport or proof of address. If you have a local cryptocurrency exchange in your own country, start applying to it first.

There are two different types of cryptocurrency exchanges and you will probably need to open an account with each:

1) Cryptocurrency exchanges that accept fiat money (regular paper money e.g. USD) to exchange for cryptocurrencies

2) Cryptocurrency exchanges that only accept coin-to-coin exchange e.g. Bitcoin for Ethereum, Bitcoin for Litecoin etc.

Steps:

1) Preferably open a cryptocurrency exchange in your country that accepts fiat money. This process can take between a few days to a few weeks. You will also most likely be asked to activate 2 Factor Authentication (2FA) which is a verification code from your smartphone every time you login for security.

2) Transfer some funds into your cryptocurrency exchange account for buying Bitcoin (BTC) or Ethereum (ETH) which are the most widely accepted coins for most ICOs.

Tip: Test first by transferring a small amount e.g. $10 or $50 into your exchange account to ensure you are sending to the right address. You don't have to buy 1 BTC or 1 ETH but a fraction as they are highly divisible and can be in amounts of 0.001 BTC or 0.018 ETH.

3) Open another cryptocurrency exchange that offers a variety of coins (these only accept coin deposits instead of fiat money).

4) After purchasing your Bitcoin or Ethereum, you can transfer them to the second exchange to buy other coins like e.g. Ripple, Litecoin, Dash etc.

Tip: If you are not interested in other altcoins, simply buy some ETH or BTC so you can participate in ICOs.

How To Select The Right Exchanges

You might have heard of Mt. Gox, an exchange in Japan that was handling 70% of all Bitcoin transactions worldwide. It unexpectedly shut down and filed for bankruptcy after reportedly missing 850,000 Bitcoins in 2014.

More recently in 2017 Youbit a cryptocurrency exchange in South Korea filed for insolvency after it was hacked twice in a year which resulted in its customers' cryptocurrency assets marked down to 70 percent of its value.

When it comes to your hard earned money, it is important to do some homework before you start trading in a particular exchange.

Checklist For Selecting Exchange:

1) Reputation

The easiest way to find out is to use our good friend Google and forums like Reddit or BitcoinTalk to search for reviews relating to the exchange you are looking at.

2) Geographical

Take note of any geographical restrictions as some exchanges might not give full access if you are from certain countries.

3) Security

Does the exchange use any 2FA and email verification?

4) Liquidity

The higher the liquidity the better it is for ease of buying and selling in the market. It also means better prices and faster transactions.

5) Coin Pairs Variety

Some exchanges like Gemini Exchange only offer popular coins like Bitcoin and Ethereum which is good enough if you are only investing in ICOs. Otherwise you might want to open an exchange account which offers a wider variety of coins for more choices.

6) Customer Support

Again look at online reviews on the quality of their customer support. You will appreciate a good and fast customer support especially if you encounter any issues with your verification process, fund transfer or trading orders.

7) Fees

Make a comparison of transaction fees on buying, selling, deposit and withdrawal etc. as all these can differ greatly from one exchange to another. Also bear in mind these transaction fees will eat into your margins especially when you become a regular trader.

Tip: Most exchanges will list their fees on their websites.

8) Exchange Rate

Do a comparison of exchange rates as it can differ as much as 10% or higher. It is a well known fact that exchanges based in South Korea are much higher due to the people's demand for Bitcoins.

Tip: Buy your Bitcoins in e.g. US but sell them in South Korea exchanges for a better price.

9) User interface

As a beginner it will help a lot if the exchange's user interface is simple to navigate to avoid any costly mistakes.

Exchanges That Accept Fiat Deposit (USD)

1) Bitstamp

Website: https://www.bitstamp.net/

Coins Available: Bitcoin, Litecoin, Ripple

Liquidity: 42 million+

Security: Average

Customer Support: Good

Trading fees: 0.25% on buying and selling

User Interface: Simple and clean

2) **Cex.IO**

Website: https://cex.io/

Coins Available: Bitcoin, Ethereum, Litecoin

Liquidity: 5 million+

Security: Average

Customer Support: Good

Trading fees: 0% Maker and 0.2% Taker

User Interface: User friendly with mobile apps

3) **GDAX**

Website: https://www.gdax.com/
Coins Available: Bitcoin, Litecoin, Ethereum

Liquidity: 97 million+

Security: High

Customer Support: Below average

Trading fees: 0% Maker and 0.25% Taker

User Interface: Simple and good

4) **Gemini**

Website: https://gemini.com/

Coins Available: Bitcoin, Ethereum
Liquidity: 57 million+

Security: High

Customer Support: Good

Trading fees: 0.25% on buying and selling

User Interface: Simple and intuitive

5) Kraken

Website: https://www.kraken.com/

Coins Available: 12 coins pairs

Liquidity: 135 million+

Security: High
Customer Support: Average

Trading fees: 0.16% Maker and 0.26% Taker

User Interface: Good

Exchanges That Accept Coin Deposit

1) Binance

Website: https:// www.binance.com/

Coins Available: 200+ coin pairs

Liquidity: 100 million+

Security: Average
Customer Support: Average

Trading fees: 0.1% on buying and selling

User Interface: Good

2) **Bitfinex**

Website: https://www.bitfinex.com/

Coins Available: 19 coin pairs

Liquidity: 120 million+

Security: Average

Customer Support: Good

Trading fees: 0.1% Maker and 0.2% Taker
User Interface: Excellent

*Requires $10,000 to open an account.

3) **Bittrex**

Website: https://bittrex.com/

Coins Available: 215 coin pairs

Liquidity: 172 million+

Security: High

Customer Support: Below average

Trading fees: 0.25% on buying and selling

User Interface: Simple

4) **Liqui**

Website: https://liqui.io/

Coins Available: 107 coin pairs

Liquidity: 17 million+

Security: Poor

Customer Support: Good

Trading fees: 0.1% Maker and 0.25% Taker

User Interface: Simple and intuitive

5) **Poloniex**

Website: https://poloniex.com

Coins Available: 90 coin pairs

Liquidity: 305 million+

Security: Average

Customer Support: Poor

Trading fees: 0.15% Maker and 0.25% Taker

User Interface: Good

Useful Resources:

Cryptocurrency Exchange Websites:

Binance: https://www.binance.com

Bitfinex: https://www.bitfinex.com/

Bitstamp: https://www.bitstamp.net/

Bittrex: https://bittrex.com/

Cex.IO: https://cex.io/

Coinbase: https://www.coinbase.com/

GDAX: https://www.gdax.com/

Gemini: https://gemini.com/

Kraken: https://www.kraken.com/
Liqui: https://liqui.io/

Poloniex: https://poloniex.com

List of ALL cryptocurrency exchanges:

https://cryptocoincharts.info/markets/info

Exchange Reviews:

- Top Ten Reviews: http://www.toptenreviews.com/money/investing/best-bitcoin-exchanges/

- Crypto Compare:
https://www.cryptocompare.com/exchanges/#/overview

- Crypto Coin Zone:
http://www.cryptocoinzone.com/bitcoin-exchange-reviews/

Google Authenticator Download for 2-step verification codes on exchanges:

Android:
https://play.google.com/store/apps/details?id=com.google.android.apps.authenticator2&hl=enb.

IOS:
https://itunes.apple.com/sg/app/googleauthenticator/id388497605?mt=8

Step 5: How To Send Your BTC or ETH To ICOs

Once you have selected the ICO you want to invest in, register your interest via their "whitelist" (or pre-sale list) to get onto their private sale before it hits the exchange for public sale. One of the advantages is there is usually a bonus of 10-30% if you invest during the private sale but there is also usually a lockup period of one to three months before you can sell your tokens.

Note: For whitelist you will be required to give an email to register your interest. This will be followed by an email with questionnaire and KYC (Know Your Customer) to pre-qualify you for the pre-sale. Upon approval for their pre-sale, you will receive a confirmation email with further instructions.

If you did not manage to get onto their whitelist, you can still register for their "crowdsale" which is also a private sale but without any bonus. The next option is to buy the tokens after it is listed on EtherDelta Exchange (https://etherdelta.com/) before it hits the other exchanges.

Note: At the time of writing, some countries like US, Canada and China are excluded from participating in ICO. Please check all information on the ICO website for their list of exclusions.

Recap:

-Whitelist (presale with bonus and maybe lockup period)

-Crowdsale (no bonus but before public sale)

-EtherDelta Exchange (before it is listed on other exchanges)

-Exchanges

Read through the ICO's guide or "Token Sale" for sending BTH or ETH to their wallet address (you can find this information on their website or blog). Make sure you follow the instructions and input the correct wallet address for payment.

Note: You will only receive your tokens at the end of the ICO which can be one to two weeks later.

IMPORTANT: DO NOT send your BTC or ETC via your exchange account as the ICO's side will NOT know who sent them. This is because the exchange address you are using is a general one and you do not control the private key (PIN). E.g. It's like you are using the public address of Starbucks to send a mail out instead of your own personal home address. Instead You **MUST** only use your own private wallets to send to ICOs.

Setting Up Your Own Private Wallet:

1) **Setting Up Bitcoin Wallet**

Website: https://blockchain.info/wallet/#/signup

a) Click "Get a Free Wallet"

b) Fill out all details as required. Use an email you check regularly and set a strong password.

c) Upon completion you will receive a confirmation email and given a Wallet ID which is the only way for you to access your wallet.

d) Backup your paraphrase by going to Dashboard > "Security Center" and select "Backup Phrase". Print the "Recovery Sheet" and write your twelve words carefully as this is the only way to restore your wallet. Keep the Recovery Sheet in a safe place.

Tip: Don't save passwords and important details on your computer which can be hacked.

e) Link your mobile number to activate the Second Factor Authentication (2FA) for enhanced security.

f) Under Dashboard:

Select "Request" to copy your BTC or ETH wallet addresses if you want to transfer BTC or ETH from your exchange.

Select "Send" when you want to send coins to the ICO's specified Address.

2) **Setting Up MyEtherWallet (MEW)**

Website: https://www.myetherwallet.com/

a) Create New Wallet.

b) Enter a strong password and Generate Wallet.

c) Save your Keystore File (in UTC/JSON format) and make a backup to be safe. Your Keystore file is needed to access your MEW together with your password and restore your wallet.

d) Save Your Private Key (it is like your PIN) and keep it somewhere safe along with a paper copy. Once it is lost, it is lost forever with no way of recovery.

Tip: Don't save your Private Key on your computer which can be hacked. Save it in an external storage like flash drive that is offline.

e) Unlock your wallet by choosing from a list of options and select "Keystore File (UTC / JSON). Enter your Password and select the Keystore file (UTC) you downloaded earlier.

f) Now you can use this wallet that supports ETH and ERC-20 tokens and participate in ICOs. But before that instruct your Exchange to send the ETH to your MEW address first.

Note: You can also buy ETH from the Coinbase exchange widget (although their exchange rate tends to be higher).

g) To send ETH to ICO select "Send Ether & Tokens" and copy the ICO's Address and enter Amount to send. Please check all details carefully before sending as the transaction cannot be reversed.

Note: For "Gas" the recommended amount is 40 to 90 Gwei. If you put too little "Gas" your transaction will be given lower priority and take a longer time. You will most likely receive payment instructions from the ICO including the recommended Gwei.

You can check the price of ETH gas here: https://ethgasstation.info/

h) Once you receive all the information from the ICO team upon completion, you can check your ICO token received. Click "View Wallet Info" and select "Token Balances". Select "Add Custom Token" and enter the details as given to you by the ICO team. After a few seconds you should be able to see your token balance.

Note: It can take up to 2 weeks for you to receive the tokens.

Tip: Always make sure you are using only wallets from official websites and check it is not a phishing website (sites that mirror other websites and steal information such as your wallet private key). Bookmark the official page to avoid phishing website.

The advantage and purpose of using a digital wallet is so that you have full control of your coins. As cited earlier with Mt. Gox exchange losing 850,000 Bitcoins, leaving your coins in exchanges leave you vulnerable to hackers and mishandling.

Wallet Terms:

Crypto or digital wallet is a software program that stores your public and private keys.

Public key is like your bank account number.

Private key is like your PIN to access your bank account (Do not reveal to anyone or carelessly put your private key instead of public key address. You can lose your coins).

Keystore File is the encrypted version of your Private Key to prevent unauthorized access.

Reminder: NEVER send coins from your exchange to participate in ICOs. The only way you can send BTC or ETH is through your own digital wallet.

Step 6: Post ICOs

Once you have received your coins there are a few things you can do:

Option 1:

Sell your coins once it is listed in an exchange and make a profit from flipping. Do not be alarmed as most ICOs will "dump" on the first day of trading on exchange and you will see a price decrease as people will flip ICOs for a quick profit. If you got your coins pre-ICO it is relatively easy to make a quick profit because of the bonus. Please understand the initial price decrease does not mean you have lost money as you bought your coins with bonus included.

Tip: If you have missed the ICO, can't participate or was undecided, the initial sell-off during the first few days is a good opportunity for you to buy the coins.

The two fastest and most common exchanges for listing ICOs are:

a) Bittrex - https://bittrex.com/

b) Liqui.io - https://liqui.io/

Note: You will need to open an account with the above exchanges to trade.

Option 2:

If your research has left you convinced the project has huge potential, you can opt to be a medium to long term investor and hold your coins. Alternatively you can hold your coins until your target price return at e.g. x2, x3, x10 of capital.

Note: Past record has shown that the returns generated from investing in ICO can generate as much as six digits percentage gains. Don't take my word for it, see statistics since ICO: https://icostats.com/roi-since-ico

Of course all investments come with risks as well which is why it is important to practice due diligence with a thorough analysis to check if the project is viable.

Option 3: Have An Exit Strategy

Whether the trade turns out good or bad, it is prudent to have an exit strategy to protect your capital.

To lock in your profits and actualize your returns, you need to exit your trade by selling off your investments at a certain point e.g. 20%, 50% or 100% gains of your capital. One of the most common problems is greed whereby people think the price will keep on rising. Since no one knows for certain, set a target for yourself and be disciplined to exit. Most importantly enjoy your gains and look for another opportunity. Don't sabotage yourself by being too greedy.

Similarly if you have made a bad trade you need to set a manual stop-loss of e.g. 25% and sell off immediately to protect your capital. Do not be emotionally attached to your trade and learn to cut your losses early so that you can conserve your capital for another opportunity.

So congratulations, there are your 6-steps action plan to your first ICO investment.

Tips:

-Start with paper trading first or you can invest as little as $50-$100 for your initial ICOs till you gain more confidence and experience.

-Monitor your cryptocurrency prices by downloading the Blockfolio app on your smartphone.

Chapter 5: Case Studies - The Good, The Bad And The Ugly

Now we will take an in-depth look at three real life case studies of ICOs and how they turned out.

Case Study 1 - The "Good"

Project: Factom

Token Name: FCT

Website: https://www.factom.com/

Market Cap in Jan 2018: $454,233,716

Starting Price in Jan 2015: $0.210281

Current Price in Jan 2018: $64.01

Rank: 66th biggest cryptocurrency in the world

Whitepaper: https://www.factom.com/devs/docs/guide/factom-white-paper-1-0

Founders: Paul Snow and David Johnston

Team: Includes software engineers and developers, analysts and marketing personnel with strong expertise in tech line and business world.

Investors:

- Bill & Melinda Gates Foundation which awarded a $500,000 grant to Factom to build a prototype digitized medical record system for the developing nations.

- Billionaire investor Tim Draper.

- Partnership with Smartrac a leading radio frequency identification (RFID) provider to create an integrated document verification and authentication system.

- Grant from US Department of Homeland Security to advance the security of digital identity for Internet of Things (IoT) devices.

Country: HQ, Austin, Texas

Project Overview:

The Project uses blockchain technology for data management and security. It specializes in supplying solutions in compliance, identity, transparent assets and securities to enterprise, government and non-profit organizations.

Competitor: Tierion which doesn't have any working protocols yet.

Summary:

Factom could be an undervalued coin with huge potential as its value will set to increase once it reaches full potential and adoption rate by major corporations. It already has a few partnerships going for it which means it is likely to be geared for the upside. Overall Factom seems to be a boring project but so far prices have been looking stable and growing steadily since inception in 2015. This project looks suitable for long-term hold.

Case Study 2 - The "Bad"

Project: TenX

Token Name: PAY

Website: https://www.tenx.tech/

Market Cap in Jan 2018: $326,199,998

Starting Price in Jun 2017: $25.22

Current Price in Jan 2018: $3.81

Rank: 92th biggest cryptocurrency in the world

Whitepaper: https://www.tenx.tech/whitepaper/tenx_whitepaper_final.pdf

Founders: Toby Hoenisch, Julian Hosp, Michael Sperk & Paul Kitti

Team: Big team including software engineers, developers, iOS and Android leads, product, marketing, legal financial, compliance personnel etc.

Investors:

- Fenbushi Capital

- ICH

Country: Singapore

Project Overview:

TenX is a payment company which offers crypto-debit card and crypto-mobile wallet funded by cryptocurrency. It has partnership with VISA and Mastercard which allows TenX card to be used in 200 countries. Cardholders can pay for purchases using Bitcoin, Ethereum, DASH and ERC20 altcoins.

Competitors: Tokencard, Mobi, Xapo and Monaco (but cards are denominated in USD, GBP and EUR)

Summary:

In theory TenX looks like a very exciting and promising project. Imagine the convenience of paying with a card that is linked to your cryptocurrencies and priced reasonably at $15 and an annual fee of $10 if the spending is above $1000 per annum. Moreover there are no transaction fees and cardholders can even earn reward of 0.1% on all transactions in TenX tokens. Who wouldn't want a TenX card?

So why did its price plunge from a promising start of $25.22 to $3.81 currently? TenX did not have any direct agreement with VISA and Mastercard but Wavecrest which is a partner of VISA and Mastercard. Unfortunately on October 2017 (four months after its launch) Wavecrest changed their service agreement such that TenX card can now only be used in European Union (EU) instead of the 200 countries promised. Currently TenX only supports Bitcoin (BTC) and Ethereum (ETH). DASH and ERC20 tokens are still on their roadmap.

TenX can still turn around if it can get a solid service agreement with VISA and Mastercard to be accepted worldwide. But in the meantime it is best to wait and see if TenX can redeem themselves or if other competitors such as FuzeX card which is launching its ICO on 15th January 2018 (at the time of writing) will overtake them.

Case Study 3 - The "Ugly"

Project: BitConnect

Token Name: BCC

Website: https://bitconnect.com/

Market Cap in Jan 2018: $1,690,862,250

Starting Price in Jan 2017: $0.162671

Current Price in Jan 2018: $290.84

Rank: 26th biggest cryptocurrency in the world

Whitepaper: Nothing found at https://bitconnect.co/tag/white-paper

Founders and Developers: No mention on website

Country Registered: Caymans Islands

Project Overview: For people to store and invest their money and earn substantial interest on their investment.

Note: Function like a MLM / Ponzi scheme. Promise investors high returns based on 1-7% referral fees. Pay previous investors with money invested by new investors.

How it claims to generate ROI: Through fictional trading bot and volatility software.

Status:

- 4 Jan 2018 served a Cease and Desist order by Texas State Securities Board.

- 17 Jan 2018 the company closed its shutter.

Warning: Re-launched as another ICO BitConnectX.

Summary:

BitConnect is a typical MLM / Ponzi scheme which offers "guaranteed return" based on a 1-7% referral system. On the website, the faceless company does not name its founders or developers and is based on Caymans Islands (infamous for hiding money and money laundering). The business appears to have no purpose, service or products except to offer an affiliate membership program whereby previous members / investors are paid by newer members / investors but with no retail products. In summary BitConnect create their own coin that is the equivalent of "printing money" out of thin air.

Conclusion

Now that you have seen the "good, bad and ugly" of ICOs, here is a reminder to practice due diligence in your ICO analysis and to understand what the project is about before investing your hard earned money. Do not be too in love with a particular ICO even when things look bad, instead be disciplined to cut your losses and safeguard your capital.

Chapter 6: Risk Management & Trading Psychology

Risk Management

Trading cryptocurrencies is the same as trading any stocks and shares. Managing your trading portfolio and knowing your risk appetite will determine how safely or actively you trade. In general it is prudent to diversify your trading portfolio rather than putting all your eggs into one basket. For example, if you put all your money into one investment and it fails, you will stand to lose your entire capital.

A sensible and recommended trading portfolio can look something like this:

1) 30-45% in base currency like Bitcoin (BTC) and Ethereum (ETH) as they are the oldest and biggest cryptocurrencies worldwide. In fact almost all ICOs require you to have ETH to invest. Their stability also means they are less volatile compared to other altcoins. You can buy BTC and ETH from any exchanges but do take note of any sudden price movements affected by major news before buying.

Tip: Use USDT Conversion (available at most exchanges) during high volatility or if you foresee some major news to protect your portfolio. For e.g. convert your BTC or ETH temporarily into USD Tether (USDT) which are tokens pegged to USD. This could be your best option during high volatility to wait out instead of constantly changing positions. You can then conveniently convert your USDT back to BTC or ETH when the market stabilizes.

Note: Only certain coins can be converted to USDT. If you hold e.g. NEO you have to convert to BTC, ETH, XRP, LTC or other compatibles before you can convert to USDT.

2) 30-35% in fundamental coins e.g. Factom (FTC). Fundamental coins are those you have identified as long-term holding coins backed by sound technology, experienced team with long term viability and prospect. You can buy these fundamental coins after they are listed on the exchanges and look promising for long term growth. For example, you can still buy FTC from any exchanges as in investment even though you did not invest at its ICO stage.

3) 20-30% in ICOs. Since these are initial coin offerings issued to the public for the first time, they also posses the highest returns and highest risk (most have no track record or working proof) which is why you might want to invest in ICOs on a smaller scale.

Actively monitor all your investments so that you are privy to any adverse volatility that might compromise your portfolio.

Tip: Download the app Blockfolio to monitor your investments. It allows you to conveniently setup price alerts, notifications and latest news at your fingertips.

Bonus Tip:

In December 2017, Bitcoin lost a quarter of its value when it plunged by 40 percent ($5000+) in five days. Ethereum dropped 36 percent and Litecoin at 43 percent. In general all cryptocurrencies fell by an average of 22 percent. This was due partly to the bearish sentiments of the crypto market as a bubble and rumored unresolved problems with Bitcoin's infrastructure.

As you can see the cryptocurrency market is extremely sensitive to news. Anything like development updates, partnerships or rumors can have a significant impact on the cryptocurrency market and affect your portfolio.

While we can't be privy to every piece of news, it is wise to know what kind of news will affect our investments. Such knowledge can becomes a risk management tool or even a trading opportunity e.g. during the December 2017 drop, many savvy investors like Julian Hosp of Tenx bought Bitcoin at a "discount" of 40 percent.

In the cryptocurrencies market, you should always be on the lookout for triggers that may affect the market or any news or new developments specific to your individual coins.

How To Decipher Potential Market Moving News Or Events:

- Government regulations or warnings e.g. On 11 Jan 2018 South Korean government threatened to issue a bill banning cryptocurrencies trading in their country causing all trading exchanges to halt temporarily = Negative

- Listing of new ICO coins into an exchange = Positive

- De-listing of coins from an exchange = Negative

- Fork announcement; soft fork, hard fork, software fork = Negative

- Announcement of partnerships or collaborations = Positive

- Market manipulation by "whales" (big money players who can potentially tank or prop the market) = Negative

Useful resources to bookmark:

1) Development Updates:

- Bitcoin (https://www.cryptocoinsnews.com/bitcoin-calendar/)

- Ethereum (https://timesofethereum.com/)

2) Exhibitions & Conventions

- http://www.coindesk.com/bitcoin-events

- https://bitcoin.org/en/events

Trading Psychology

All forms of investing and trading are psychological and emotional for most people because it involves our hard earned money. Making money in the cryptocurrency market without taking the time to understand its technology and fundamentals will also cause you to second guess your investment choices and self sabotage. While you do not need to be a technical geek, do invest some time reading up on, for example, how cryptocurrencies work, blockchains, smart contracts, POW, POS, hard forks, meaning of decentralized etc., or anything of interest to you. Any additional knowledge will definitely make you a savvier investor than the next guy who is just rushing in to make a quick buck without understanding anything.

As you advance in your trading journey, here are some common emotions you will most likely experience:

1) **FUD (Fear, Uncertainty and Doubt)**

In a typical FUD scenario, it is normally caused by bad news or negative market sentiments. The reason prices plummet or soar suddenly has nothing much to do with fundamentals but people's emotions getting out of hand. Typical FUD situations:

- JPMorgan's CEO Jamie Dimon spread FUD by saying Bitcoin is a "fraud" that will eventually blow up

- Jan 2018 the market reacted negatively to the news China is curbing their Bitcoin miners which accounts for 60 percent worldwide

- Jan 2018 South Korean government threatening to release a bill banning cryptocurrency trading (30 percent of working adults in South Korea own cryptocurrencies)

- Missed roadmaps targets and deadlines by certain project

- Partnerships fallout

- False rumors and fake news

- Personal incorrect market analysis

2) FOMO (Fear Of Missing Out)

This is the fear of missing out a "good deal" and following the masses blindly when making investment decisions. Perhaps you have a trading plan and have done your proper analysis checklist but you heard a fantastic deal on the forum about another upcoming ICO. FOMO overcomes you and you end up chasing every ICO / coin instead of sticking to your trading plan because you are afraid to miss out.

3) Your Worst Enemy - Greed

It is very easy to be overcome by greed especially in cryptocurrency when one can stand to make a few hundred percent over. Remember it is only a paper gain till you cash out your profits. Being a good trader means having a specific target at e.g. 100% of gains. Sell and enjoy your profits instead of regretting when the market turns against you.

Conclusion

While we cannot control market sentiments and behavior, we can learn to manage our own psychology and emotions by:

- Always practice due diligence and do your own research and analysis so you won't be affected by FUD

- Do not engage in FOMO and chase after every "opportunity"

- Always listen to outside news and opinions with a pinch of salt

- Checking news regularly does not mean you should obsess over every bit of information

- Have an exit strategy e.g. converting your coins into USDT temporarily in a volatile market

- Tame your inner greed by having a specific target e.g. 100% gains and be disciplined to stick to it

- When your coin is down, don't panic and try to remember the market does not go in one direction only but also up and down. Oftentimes it is a temporary market correction, so be patient for your coin to recover

- Be patient and wait for the right time, or rather price, to buy your coins. For e.g. the best time to buy is when the market crashes and everything is on "discount"

- Trade only money you can afford to lose and do not borrow or put your house on mortgage hoping you will "strike gold" as this will only put additional stress on you

- Lastly, if you have made a trading error, adopt a growth mindset to learn from your mistake and do better next time.

Chapter 7: Bonus

Types Of Crypto Wallets

In the earlier chapter we covered online wallets for your Bitcoin and Ethereum but now we will look at other types of crypto wallets and the differences.

The difference between hot and cold wallet is simply if it is connected to the internet. Hot wallets like online wallets are less secure as they can be hacked. Cold wallets or cold storage such as paper wallet or hardware wallets are more secure as they are stored offline like a real life safe where you keep your valuables.

1) Mobile wallets are apps installed on your smartphone allowing you to send, receive and transact cryptocurrencies on the go.

For IOS and Android:

- Airbitz
- Bitcoin wallet
- Bither
- BreadWallet
- Coinomi
- Copay
- CoinSpace
- Electrum
- GreenAddress
- GreenBits
- MyCelium

- Simple Bitcoin

2) Online Wallets let you access your wallet over a web browser. They are also most risky to hacking.

- Coinbase wallet
- Bitalo web-only wallet
- BitGo web wallet
- Blockchain.info wallet
- MEW MyEtherWallet

3) Desktop Wallets is a software that is installed on your computer. It can be very safe if the computer does not connect to the internet and is only used for storing cryptocurrencies.

- Bitcoin Core
- Electrum desktop wallet
- MutiBit HD
- Exodus
- mSIGNA
- CoPay

4) Paper Wallets are physical paper documents that contain your public and private keys as well as QR codes that can be scanned during transactions. Such wallets are very safe as they are stored offline and ideal for beginners as they do not require any technical skills to run.

- BitAddress.org
- LiteAddress.org
- ETHAddress

5) Hardware Wallets are more secure than hot wallets as they are offline devices that can't be hacked. It can even be used safely on malware infected computers. This is highly recommended and an absolute must if you hold large quantities of cryptocurrencies, due to its strong security feature. Some look like flash drives and come with screens and tiny buttons.

- Trezor
- Ledger Nano
- KeepKey

No matter which wallet you prefer, remember your cryptocurrencies are only safe if your private keys are generated securely and kept secret. As your investment portfolio grows, you will want to keep your coins in a secure place and it is not prudent to leave your coins in exchanges which can be hacked or compromised as mentioned in earlier chapters.

How To Transfer Coins

As your cryptocurrency trading progresses, you will most likely be holding different coins in different exchange accounts and use different cryptocurrency wallets. To buy and sell coins, you will likely need to transfer coins from one exchange to another account or wallets. The steps are generally similar from one exchange or wallet to another.

1. Login to your exchange account e.g. Gemini Exchange

2. Look for "Wallet" section

3. Click at the coin you want e.g. Bitcoin and select "Withdraw"

4. Enter carefully the receiving address (e.g. exchange or wallet address) to send your Bitcoin to

Note: To find the receiving address Click "Deposit" or the "+" symbol on your receiving exchange or wallet e.g. Binance Exchange and copy address or use the QR code shown.

QR Code

5. Paste it onto your sending account e.g. Gemini Exchange and click "Withdraw"

6. Check if you receive an email from your exchange to confirm the withdrawal

To check if your Bitcoin transfer went through:

Copy and paste your Transaction ID (TxID) or exchange or wallet address into:

https://blockchain.info/

Or

To check if your Ethereum transfer went through:

Copy and paste your Transaction ID (TxID) or exchange or wallet address into:

http://etherscan.io/

All your transaction details will show up after awhile as this is the beauty of blockchain whereby everything is transparent and online.

Note: Try to do your transfers between Mondays to Fridays as some exchanges will only transfer your coins on Mondays when they are open.

Tip: Test with a small amount first to make sure you got every step correct as the transaction is irreversible.

Conclusion

Thank you for taking massive action to educate yourself in the world of trading cryptocurrencies. Now you know a lot more than the majority who only recognize Bitcoin as a digital currency.

The action plan and steps you have learned have been tested and proven to create results. The action plan set out for you here is simple, and the results available to anyone who is prepared to put in the work. Follow the plan and commit to a journey towards the best life you can imagine.

In the meantime continue to educate yourself in the world of cryptocurrency and always trade with caution. Making mistakes is human so always instill in yourself a growth mindset to learn and be wiser next time.

Fast forward a few years and you might be one of those who have semi-retired early and telling others it is because you took action and invested early in cryptocurrency years ago while others were still sitting on the fence or too lazy to find out more, thinking it was just a hype.

To your success,

-- Kate C.

P.S. I'll be most grateful if you can kindly leave a supportive review on Amazon and share what you liked. Your testimonials are what will help to make the next version even better. Thank you so much!

Useful Resources

Information on ICOs

- Crush Crypto: https://crushcrypto.com/
- Smith & Crown: https://www.smithandcrown.com/
- ICO Alert: https://www.icoalert.com/
- Reddit Channels: /r/Cryptocurrency and /r/icocrypto

Cryptocurrency News

-Reddit: https://www.reddit.com
- r/icocrypto (Channel for Initial Coin Offerings)
- r/cryptocurrency (Channel on all cryptocurrencies)
- Steemit: https://steemit.com
- BitcoinForum: https://bitcointalk.org
- Twitter: www.twitter.com
- Slack: www.slack.com/

Development Updates

- Bitcoin: https://www.cryptocoinsnews.com/bitcoin-calendar/
- Ethereum: https://timesofethereum.com/

Cryptocurrency Events

- https://bitcoin.org/en/events
- http://www.coindesk.com/bitcoin-events

Cryptocurrency Exchange Websites

- Binance: https://www.binance.com
- Bitfinex: https://www.bitfinex.com/

- Bitstamp: https://www.bitstamp.net/
- Bittrex: https://bittrex.com/
- Cex.IO: https://cex.io/
- Coinbase: https://www.coinbase.com/
- GDAX: https://www.gdax.com/
- Gemini: https://gemini.com/
- Kraken: https://www.kraken.com/
- Liqui: https://liqui.io/
- Poloniex: https://poloniex.com

List of ALL cryptocurrency exchanges: https://cryptocoincharts.info/markets/info

Review of Exchanges

- Top Ten Reviews: http://www.toptenreviews.com/money/investing/best-bitcoin-exchanges/
- Crypto Compare: https://www.cryptocompare.com/exchanges/#/overview
- Crypto Coin Zone: http://www.cryptocoinzone.com/bitcoin-exchange-reviews/

Google Authenticator Download for 2-step verification codes on exchanges

Android: https://play.google.com/store/apps/details?id=com.google.android.apps.authenticator2&hl=enb.
IOS: https://itunes.apple.com/sg/app/googleauthenticator/id388497605?mt=8

Bitcoin Wallets

-Web Based: Blockchain.info: https://blockchain.info/wallet/#/signup
Paper Wallet:
- Bitcoin Paper Wallet: https://bitcoinpaperwallet.com
- BitAdress: https://www.bitaddress.org/bitaddress.org

Ethereum Wallets

- Web Based: My Ether Wallet: https://www.myetherwallet.com

List of ERC-20 Tokens: https://etherscan.io/tokens

Others

- Statistics Since ICO: https://icostats.com/roi-since-ico
- Measuring Liquidity: https://coinmarketcap.com/
- Blockfolio App Download:
Android: https://play.google.com/store/apps/details?id=com.google.android.apps.authenticator2&hl=eno
IOS: https://itunes.apple.com/sg/app/googleauthenticator/id388497605?mt=8
- Verify Your Bitcoin Transactions: https://blockchain.info/
- Verify Your Ethereum Transaction: http://etherscan.io/
- Bitcoin White Paper: https://bitcoin.org/bitcoin.pdf

www.ingramcontent.com/pod-product-compliance
Lightning Source LLC
Chambersburg PA
CBHW070317230526
45470CB00002B/919